To Barb,
A prayer Fo
reason.
God Bless you!
Henri P—
Psalm 121

Straight from the Heart

Straight from the Heart
Prayers for Everyday Living

Holli Pearson

Prairie Prayers
MINISTRIES
STILWELL, KANSAS

Straight from the Heart: Prayers for Everyday Living

Copyright © 2008 by Prairie Prayers Ministries

Interior and Cover Design: Christy Kelley

Photo Credits: Mr. Sidney McKnight

ISBN 978-0-9822429-0-2

00 01 02 03 04 — 19 18 17 16 15
Printed in the United States of America

Dedication

I give all the praise, glory and honor to the Lord God Almighty who instilled this passion for prayer in me at a very young age. I would first like to thank my family, my husband Steve, who is so very good to me and blesses me with both his love and support; my two beautiful boys, Pete, his wife Amy, and Joe, who at times, do not really understand what I am doing but support me anyway. I also would like to acknowledge the following people who continually encourage me to write; Carol McKnight, my mentor and prayer partner; Betty Maes, my other prayer partner; Shari Wilkins; Jeanne Dreiling; and Susie Schweiker, the sister of my heart. I am ever thankful for Church of the Resurrection, Senior Pastor Adam Hamilton and Michelle Funk, the head of Women's Ministries, who surround me with encouragement and support. Many, many heartfelt thanks to Deb Fechter, my right arm, who has helped me edit and re-write again and again; Christy Kelley whose designs truly give glory to God; Kelly Synder, whose business wisdom was the guiding force in putting this all together; and lastly Trojan Press, for the effortless way they made this all happen. God truly has put together a wonderful team and we give all the glory to Him! Your patience and endurance is a blessing to me.

Foreword

Some find the reading of prayers written by others to be superficial, or somehow artificial. They believe unless one uses his or her own words, offered extemporaneously without prior thought, the prayer is somehow invalid. But the ancient Israelites did not think this to be so. They collected and published prayers that were particularly helpful or meaningful, and they would turn to these prayers again and again for comfort, help or guidance. These prayers gave voice to the thoughts and yearnings of generations of Israelites. We know these prayers as the Book of Psalms.

People of faith composed the Psalms as they walked through the various seasons of life. They include hymns filled with exuberant joy ("Bless the Lord, O my soul, and all that is within me bless God's holy name!"). Yet, they also include laments or complaints uttered in dark times when faith was hard to come by ("How long, O Lord? Will you forget me forever?"). We love them because they help us communicate what we feel but might not find words to express. This is as God intended and in this we see the Spirit's inspiration and hear God's word.

Like the Psalmists, Holli Pearson has captured, in this volume of prayers, the full range of our human experience — joy and sorrow, exuberance and emptiness, despair and hope. She puts into words what many of us feel at various times, even as her prayers help us reflect upon the meaning of our lives.

These prayers could be read as poetry, pondered as small sermons, viewed as autobiographically as windows into the life of one particular follower of Jesus. But they could also be conceived as the starting point for the reader's own conversations with God, leading us to express our own struggles and heartaches, blessings and joys.

I am honored to be Holli's pastor. I have seen the sincerity of her faith and the seriousness with which she takes prayer. It is her hope in publishing this book, that it brings glory to God and blesses the reader. I believe you will agree she has accomplished her objectives.

Rev. Adam Hamilton

Acknowledgements

Prayer is the avenue available to us to communicate with God. We talk to Him with words of praise, thanksgiving, and joy; we also share our feelings of worry, anxiety, and sorrow. Holli Pearson has answered God's calling to pen honest and sincere prayers to a God who desires to hear what is on our hearts.

Holli serves in a variety of ways at The United Methodist Church of the Resurrection. She is the Prayer Chair for Women's Ministry at Resurrection and leads a weekly group during a time of corporate prayer. She teaches Bible studies that focus on prayer as well as on various books and characters of the Bible. Holli is part of a home-based small group and fosters authentic fellowship among the members.

This collection of prayers will become personal to those who read it. They will be able to grow in their prayer life as they experience the words of Holli. Readers will find these words lingering in their minds even after they have put down Holli's book. I look forward to seeing these beautiful prayers published and available to all!

Michelle Funk
Director of Women's Ministry
United Methodist Church of the Resurrection

Introduction

What are prayers for everyday living? They are conversations with God on what we need to get through the day. We ask God to guide, protect, direct, and provide for us each day. Prayer cements our relationship with God, who sustains our continuity. It is through our relationship with God, that we find our purpose and direction for our lives. Prayer is a part of our walk with God. It is through communicating with God, reading His Word, and praying, that we find peace in our life and with God.

This book is setup to reflect a season you might be experiencing in your life. Spring prayers are meant for the times in your life of growth, new possibilities, new opportunities, and excitement about the future. Summer prayers reflect a time for contentment, peace, and finding rest in the joys that God has given you. Fall prayers are filled with transition, change, and uncertainties. A time to re-focus and re-dedicate your life to Christ. Winter marks a time of trials, difficulties, solitude, and discouragement; knowing that through Christ, our comforter, you will be guided to a new season.

Prayer is not difficult. There is no special formula. It is just talking to God. He loves you, always and forever. He wants a relationship with you and prayer is one of the most important parts of this relationship. Find a prayer that speaks to you, according to the season of life you may be in, and pray. Prayer becomes easier by practicing it. Continue praying with faith, knowing that your prayers, no matter how short or simple, have been heard. God desires to hear from you and delights in you when you pray.

Remember:

Psalm 34:7
"Take delight in the LORD
and He will give you the desires of your heart."

Colossians 4:2
Devote yourselves to prayer, being watchful and thankful."

I Thessalonians 5:16–18
"Rejoice always, pray continually, give thanks in all circumstances; for this is God's will for you in Christ Jesus."

Table of Contents

$\mathcal{F}_{all}\,\mathcal{P}_{rayers}$

$\mathcal{W}_{inter}\,\mathcal{P}_{rayers}$

Spring

Achievement

Dear Father God, Jesus Christ, and the Holy Spirit,

You, Lord, are my salvation, my life, my world!
I am nothing without You and
everything with You!

I pray for direction, guidance,
and the awesome power and might of Your son Jesus Christ,
to achieve according to Your will,
the goals You have set before me!

Holy Lord, the battle is Yours!
Clear the path of the obstacles I should not see
and help me to step over, in peace,
the ones I need to learn from.
As impossible as this task seems, Lord God,
I trust in Your word that says,
You are able to do more than what I ask or imagine,
according to Your power that is at work within me!"

Help me to activate that power,
to go down Your chosen path,
to be obedient to Your will.

I pray to succeed in this endeavor,
Holy Father God,
but not with any self-centered achievement,
pride, or ego,
but always to You be the glory
in Your Church and in Your son, Christ Jesus,
throughout all generations forever and ever!

Amen

Birthday Blessings

O, Father God,

Thank You, Lord,
for another birthday.
Another day to see Your beauty.
Another day to feel the sun,
notice the stars,
and feel the love of family.

Thank You, Lord,
for my beautiful family,
that through trials and tribulations,
we constantly and consistently
see each other through.

I thank You, Lord,
for another day of birds singing,
teenagers telephones ringing,
and the gifts of friendship.

Thank You most of all, Lord,
for choosing me
and thinking I am worthy
and showing me Your purpose.

Your love, God,
sustains me and guides me.
May my life be an offering of praise to You.

Amen

Failure

Dear Lord God,

I struggle so with failure;
perfection at all times seems to be my goal.

It is in the humbling of my failure and my own ineptitude,
that I reach out to You the most.

Strength in faith is not built on success
but on continuous climbs out of the gutter,
of repeated trials at life.

During the trials of my life,
I sense and become aware of Your presence and strength.
I long for Your shield to hide behind,
so that I may rise from the ashes of Your sacrifice
to the light of the living.

Help me, Lord God,
to renew my soul,
fill my spirit with the hope of new possibilities
and the future tasks You have assigned to me.

I want to remember I do not live an unblemished life.
That it is in the fires of living,
that I learn to rely on You as my guide,
teacher, and deliverer.
That You, Christ Jesus…
my Atonement, my Holy Spirit Guide,
is with me always.

Help me open my heart and mind,
and fill me with the hope of You in all of my tomorrows.

Amen

Faith

Dear Lord,

I pray for faith!
To walk obediently,
live in peace,
knowing You are in control,
and that all the events in my life happen
according to Your timetable.

Help me to see the signs,
of when to be still
and when I should run towards
all that You have planned for me.

I pray I would never be disappointed,
in any circumstance,
but reside in hope,
that You, God,
will work for Your glory
and my eternal benefit.

Hope does not disappoint!
I choose to live hopeful!
Lord God, all that I am, I give to You…
to guide, protect,
and serve with joy.

I choose to live faithfully.
I hope to live joyfully,
trusting in You, always.

Amen

Gentle and Teachable Spirit

Dear Lord Jesus,

I surrender and submit my life
to You this day.
I pray You will help me to develop
an inward grace of my soul.

I pray I will never boast
or let pride and my ego take control.
Help me to stay humble
filled with Your Holy Spirit.

I hope to think of others,
before myself.
To serve, encourage, guide
and pray for others continually.

Let my focus and thoughts
dwell on being approachable,
teachable and obedient
to what Your Word professes.

I bow down before You;
willing to learn, seeking Your face.
Build in me, Father God,
a gentleness of spirit
through the awesome power
of Your son, Jesus Christ.

Amen

Grace

Dear Lord Jesus,

I need to forgive them for hurting my feelings,
for years of neglect
and loss of fellowship.

You tell me to forgive if I expect to be forgiven.
That "if" is what motivates me,
I want desperately to be forgiven.
I know I am a sinner, I am very imperfect.

I am like the prodigal son, Lord.
I have worked hard for You…
did You notice me?
Why would You celebrate this lost soul and ignore me?

If I want mercy from You,
I must also give mercy and grace.
Because my faith is not based on works,
but on mercy!

This is a hard lesson for me, Lord!
To practice forgiveness, mercy,
and grace with no boundaries.
It is the lesson You are longing to teach me,
that I still have yet to perfect!

I am learning about grace,
there is freedom from judgment, anger, and frustrations.
The bitterness and list of grievances
I have piled up are blown away
by the breadth of Your love.

I pray earnestly that each day,
I will learn to forgive and love like You,
my merciful and loving Lord.

Thank You, Lord,
for one more life lesson.
I pray I will be open to more.

Amen

Guide This Day

Dear Lord, the Father of Creation, Your Son Jesus Christ
and the Holy Spirit,

Please open my heart and soul
as I walk through this day to see Your work,
in both the details and the big picture.

In setting my goals, Lord,
I seek Your direction,
Your path.
I do not seek my own understanding
but Your wisdom.

Help me, Lord,
to see my talents, given to me by You,
and to use them to Your glory,
without fear; boldly!

I repent my sins of impatience and selfishness
with the desire for a clean and pure heart.
I empty myself
so that I may be filled by You, O Christ.

May I keep my heart lifted
and listen to Your presence, Lord.
Fill me with Your peace of mind
and help me walk today with the overflowing joy
of Your salvation.

Amen

I Believe

Marriage and children, Lord,
what were You thinking?
That somehow, only through Your power,
I would do it all right?

I fail miserably!
My husband knows I am not nearly as holy
as others believe I am.
My children act flabbergasted
at my bursts of anger and temper.
I am appalled at my lack of self-control and love.

I do everything I know to be wrong, according to Your Word!
But in knowing Your Word,
I follow in the steps of the apostle Paul,
who also fell short, yet claimed Your covering of the cross.

I claim the cross too!
I believe Jesus Christ is Your Son who died for my sins.
I believe Jesus intercedes to You,
on my behalf,
with every prayer I utter.

I believe in eternal life through my faith
in the Holy Trinity.
I believe You are my guide through this often trouble-filled life,
if I let Your Spirit lead and look for Your signs.

I believe anything bad is temporary and all good is eternal
because You, God,
created this beautiful world.

I believe when I die,
I will have no regrets.
I gave my life to You, Lord,
and together we did the best!

I believe when I am finally and eternally
with You, Lord,
my life will seem so small and Your glory
so magnificent!

Thank You for this life, for my husband,
for my children.
It is a blessed life!

Amen

Intercession, Hope, and Miracles

Dear Jesus the Christ, the One and Only,

Open wide my heart and mind
to this very important day.
Expand my belief and faith beyond
what I ask or imagine.

Help me to go boldly, asking in faith,
perseverance, hope and in Your name, Jesus,
against the powers of any evil
and open the flood gates to signs,
wonders, and miracles.

Open my eyes to Your whispers in this coming week.
May I notice all big and small miracles.
Praise Your Holy Name!
Hosanna in the Highest!

May this bold step of faith,
not falter or stumble,
but stand strong with Your armor, God,
filled with Your Holy Spirit,
blessed and guided by You, Lord Jesus Christ,
the One and Only.

Amen

I See Your Presence, Lord!

I see Your presence, Lord,
in the early Spring morning with the birds singing
with the geese calling and flying over my home.

I see Your presence, Lord,
in the laughter around the kitchen table;
the joy of being a family.

I see Your presence, Lord,
in the sunshine and warmth of the Spring days.

I see Your presence, Lord,
in answered prayers to urgent needs
and in unanswered prayers,
that are waiting for direction.

I see Your presence, Lord,
in the tears of betrayal, the valleys of trials
that make me stronger and see more clearly
what You want me to become...
for You.

I see Your presence, Lord,
in babies, puppies, and butterflies,
all innocent and peaceful.

I see Your presence, Lord,
in my renewed spirit and repentant heart.
I see Your presence, Lord,
every day, every moment,
if I look for it.

Amen

Joy

Dear Lord,

Restore my joy!
Though the world throws all negative words, actions,
and ideas at me,
plant in me the faithfulness to stand strongly
in the knowledge that joy comes shining
through the door of difficulty.

I pray to remember that difficulty, distress, and frustration
can be joy stealers, however,
if I look at these situations with Christ-like eyes,
I remember that if You ordained any of it —
even if You have not…
You will restore my joy and my soul.

My salvation, my relationship with You, Lord,
and my fellowship with other believers are my joy.
Abiding in You is my joy.
You did not ordain my life to be damaged,
hurtful, or faithless.

You gave me Your Word…
Your many promises,
that through the dark and dreary trials,
You will stay with me, hold me up…
Help me to see Your light and long to stay close to it.

So I pray this day,
to be filled with Your presence and purpose.
I pray I will hear Your gentle whispers.
To be full of joy because of what I believe.
I stand on Your faithfulness and Your promise
of continued restoration!

May I focus on my joy of You and my joy in You, My Lord.
Help me to be a joy keeper!

Amen

Lost Friend

Dear Lord God,

I worry about my friend who seems so lost!
She knows you, Lord,
but she is so afraid to let go of this world
and grab hold of you!

I pray she could know the peace that comes from looking
to You for guidance and answers.

Knowing that when the answers are not given,
she is to wait and look for direction from You,
not from herself.

It is this peace that lives in my soul
that comes from keeping and staying close to You, God,
that I pray she would know!

I pray she would come to You,
with a faith that moves mountains
and that she would know that the peace in her soul only
comes from surrendering all to You!

I pray she would have the courage and energy
to give You her every burden.

I pray she would know You as I do,
and that You, God,
would reveal Yourself to her in ways that I cannot even imagine.
I stand in persevering faith and I know
You are working in her.

Help me to be Your servant
with words of faith and wisdom
so that she will witness and acknowledge
Your presence and purpose in her life!

Amen

El Shaddai, God Almighty

You are El Shaddai, the God of the mighty universe,
creator of all.
You are the God of promises and covenants.
The God who sees.
Your Word is eternal and Your
Holy Spirit is my guide.

What is in a name?
Your name defines the creation.
You are my Savior, You save and redeem.
You are the vine, and as a branch,
I must stay attached to You…to grow

I AM is the great I AM
You are a jealous God.
You desire my full attention.

What is in a name?
Everything I need.
My Mighty God, My Provider,
Counselor, Savior, Healer, Father
The God who knows.

El Shaddai, God Almighty,
I worship You and praise Your Holy, Holy Name.
Let me remember my name…
Yours, chosen, adopted, accepted, received, forgiven, loved.

Let me cry out to You, the God I need,
for the very breath and strength
necessary for each day.
Your Word, Your promises and Your love,
will hold me close.

El Shaddai, God Almighty
You are the King of the Universe.
Be my King, rule my heart,
save my soul.

What is in a name?
Everything! Everything I need!

Amen

Overwhelmed

Holy Father God, the Almighty, Your Son,
Jesus Christ, and the Holy Spirit,

Today I am overwhelmed,
by what is expected of me,
by what needs to be done.

Today, Lord,
I want so badly to bask in Your love,
not run a million errands
and talk to cranky people.

Today, I am overwhelmed
by my selfishness and laziness.
I am tired, Lord.

Please, Lord,
renew my soul.
Fill me with the energy necessary
to do the tasks You want done today.

May I greet everyone today
as Your servant,
full of love and compassion.

As Your servant,
May I serve.

Amen

Lead in Love

I want to lead in love, Lord
to take no offense, no hurt,
onto my shoulders or into my heart.
I choose to love, forgive
as You always love and forgive me.

I hope to keep my focus on love,
Your never ending, never forsaking love.
Disappointment and discouragement
are my enemies, burdens I do not need.

Let me exchange Your beauty
for the world's ashes.
To remember the wildflower,
growing out of the rock towards the sun.

Pushing uphill at times, against forces
that want to crush me.
Leading in love, Your love,
that equips me, enables me and strengthens me.

For I know that Your love
penetrates my soul,
frees me from offense,
leaving the consequences to You, God.

I walk the path You have put before me,
not complaining, when the way is hard.
Knowing, counting on and trusting in You, God,
my Lord, my Provider of all that I need.
You will deliver me, get me through.

Leading in love is what You have called me to do,
serving others in Your love, giving freely.
This is my purpose, my want;
faith and listening to Your Holy Spirit is the way.

Love leading my way, is the life I choose.
Dwelling in peace and joy that comes from such love.
Obeying You, God; trusting all the consequences to You.
Resting in Your peace, I lead in love.

Amen

Slow Down

Dear Lord,

Help me to slow down and smell the roses,
see the sunset,
not hurry past these gifts.

I pray to become aware of Your Holy Spirit's
presence and direction.
To be obedient to it, to live in Your Spirit,
be led by Your Spirit, be filled, and keep in step
with Your Holy Spirit.

Help me to be a deeply spiritual person
who feels the pain of others,
listens with a sympathetic heart,
and sees what I can do to help others.

I need to remember that if I put You first each day,
I will accomplish what You think is important.

Keep my spiritual life in line, Lord,
with Your desires for my life.

May I live joyfully and peaceably with patience,
gentleness, self-control,
and love faithfully all the days of my life.

Amen

Spiritually Mature

Dear God the Father, Jesus Christ, and the Holy Spirit

Please fill my soul to the brim with Your Holy Spirit!
Help me to empty out all the needless distractions
of this world and allow me
to be the true fruit of Your Spirit.

I pray to be led by Your Spirit,
and become spiritually mature!
I long to feel Your love,
and in turn, express it well to others…
unconditionally as You have to me!

I joyfully hope to serve You, God
and deliver Your message, Your Word,
to Your people with believable joy!

Peace beyond my understanding is Your promise to me!
Let me explain it and live it so that others,
by my example,
will yearn for it.

Help me to be patient with the world's demands, trials
and interruptions, O God.
Patient when I sin, fail,
and do the very things I do not want to do!
Patient with the struggle of living for You,
with You, and in You.

I pray to be still…
To hear Your voice, see Your path,
be filled with Your grace.

Let me extend Your kindness and goodness,
through the filling of Your Holy Spirit,
to everyone You choose me to encounter.

Help me to be one of Your chosen people,
called by Your name.
Fill me up with Your Holy Spirit's presence,
and character this day and forevermore!

Amen

Give Freely

Help me, Lord,
not to shortchange You,
or keep from You anything that is Yours.

In thanksgiving,
I acknowledge all is Yours,
I am just passing through.

I give You all my possessions;
they are all Yours.

All that I have are gifts given by You—
I hope I have acknowledged them as such.
The many blessings of home,
food, family, and Your word,
I thank You.
I am overwhelmed by how much
You have given me.

Show me, Lord,
the ways I can give back to You.
Open my eyes to the work You have planned for me.
I pray I will do it willingly and joyfully.
Reveal to me, Lord,
what, where, and when to give.

I pray for Your provision, direction,
and obedience to You, always.

Amen

Summer

A Prayer for Healing

Holy Father God, Sanctified Jesus Christ,
and Blessed Holy Spirit,

Hear my plea, O God, for healing, physical and spiritual,
on behalf of _____.

Lord God,
I stand on the solid rock foundation of faith in You
and faith in what You can do!

In this faith, Lord, and with the Hosts of Heaven,
I pray their battle will be won.

I pray their healing will be according to Your will
and Your desires for _____'s life.

May all glory, honor and praise be to You, O, God.
I place _____ in the palm of Your hand.
Hold them close and in Your blessed name, Jesus,
I pray that by Your stripes, _____ will be healed!

Thank You, Lord Jesus,
that I can come to You
and that You hear my pleas for _____.

Thank You, Lord Jesus,
for the honor of being able to walk with You.
In this situation and in all others,
I pray my words, thoughts and actions will
continually glorify You as I seek
forever to serve You, Lord.

Amen

Believe God

I trust in You, God,
and will not be afraid.
I lay my burdens on the altar
of sacrifice and thanksgiving.

I leave it;
I will not grab it back
I lay it down, give it up, let it go!

If I really believe Your Word,
trust it, count on it!
I live victoriously, Christ-like.

Doubt has fled, replaced by a mind
that believes You, God,
and every one of Your promises.
I will build a foundation with them.

Righteousness will be Your namesake.
Grace and Your eternal mercy,
guides me to seek You and Your approval.
Others approval is insignificant and unnecessary!

I trust in You, God,
and leave fear behind.
Remember those burdens I have given to You,
heard and laid to rest!

You, Oh Lord, are the blessed controller of all things,
in the universe.
I trust and believe You.
I lay it all on the altar, let it go, walk away.
Peace will find me!

Thank You God, for teaching me
how to really believe You,
trust in You,
and receive You!

Amen

Be Still

Be still and know that I am God.
I am the Mighty Conqueror;
do not put Me in a box!

It may seem that there is no specific purpose
for you in My kingdom.
Be still and know that I am God.

I am working great things through your very existence.
Others see faith in you,
perseverance without question,
strength without worry.

Be still and know that I am God.
There will be powerful answers to prayer
on My time, and in My time,
not yours.

Be still and know that I am God.
You are My creation.
I love you with an everlasting,
unfailing, merciful,
and compassionate love.
You are a great work of art.
You are Mine!

Do not grow weary or impatient
in running the race set before you.
There are plans for your greatness in My kingdom.
But first you must learn humility,
walk in patience,
practice gentleness and kindness,
grow in faith and love always.

Be still and know that I am God.
I am Lord of Lords, King of Kings,
I will reign forever,
come with Me into eternity!

Amen

Daily

I trust in You, Father God,
to see me through times of disappointment
and disillusion,
that these times would be brief.
In the quiet times, chaotic messes,
angered moments,
You convict my soul.

I pray constantly for Your guidance.
Your Word guides my path at
the times my sin rebels;
Your Holy Spirit brings me back.

You are my hope, my life.
Joy is a life lived close to You.
Failure is turned into learning;
I am convicted and led.

Draw me near to You;
fill the holes with love.
Help me to forgive always,
You always forgive.

Help me to remember,
Your word, Your way.
To live it, to walk it, to talk it,
everywhere, every day!

Amen

Declare the Joy of the Lord

I declare the joy of You, Lord,
in the land of the living
as Your child I will live, as I believe,
filled with the joy in what I know to be true.

I am redeemed, forgiven, chosen, and loved.
You knew me in my mother's womb.
There were plans made, purpose set forth.

Your Spirit, Lord, surrounds me
and reveals to me,
all the possibilities if…
I chose You…declare You,
my Lord and my God.

There is joy in You, Lord,
in the land of the living.
If I chose to live in the light
and love all that You are.

There will be trials and adversities.
These come with living.
Change, a never ending cycle, is a part of life,
an adaptation, adjustment.

Help me to not lose the light and love of Your Spirit,
of Your loving Son, Christ Jesus, living God.
I long to cling to You, hold tight.
Stead my turbulence, I will stand firm!

I declare the joy of You, Lord,
in the land of the living.
I will walk in Your peace,
of what I know to be true.

My faithfulness will build,
as I press on toward the future,
not looking back.
What blessings will be mine,
counted as righteousness!

I declare the joy of You, Lord,
in the land of the living.
To those who believe,
walk faithfully, joyfully, confidently
filled with Your peace.

Amen

Restoration Joy

Lord God Almighty,

I pray, I may approach the throne of grace,
I plead for Your mercy.
Refreshing, renewal.
I need restoration, Lord, all the way through.

Erase the disappointments, the past regrets.
Takeaway the sins committed
knowingly, imperfectly.

Fill me with Your presence.
Anoint me with Your peace.
Peace that comes with understanding,
knowing that I am Your child.

You have redeemed me, loved me, forgiven me.
I pray my life, my walk,
will be worthy of Your sacrifice.

May I never take Your sacrifice lightly.
I long to make a difference,
in the lives of those You put in my path.
Defining my purpose, as I walk closer to You.

Restoration joy, Lord,
fill me to the brim.
Focused on You, on Your plan for me.

Let me keep pressing forward
to the life, the plan, You have for me.
Keep my feet directed, energized.

Oh, the joy of a life lived with purpose.
Overwhelming love for You, God.
Love for others, gratitude, thankfulness.

Thank You, God,
for who you are in my life.
Let me not miss a minute,
of all that You are doing and will do.

Restoration joy, Lord,
receiving Your favor and lavish love.
Let me always and forever,
delight myself in You.

Amen

Husband

Thank You, Lord,
for my husband,
whom You picked just for me!
Thank You that he sees my flaws
and helps me laugh at them.

Thank You, Lord,
for my husband,
who after all these years,
really does listen and care.
Who tells me that what I am doing as his wife
and mother of his children,
is so important!

Thank You for the longing to grow old
with this man.
Thank You, Lord,
for his faith,
which seems to take over when mine waivers.

Thank You, Lord,
for all the laughter, tears and fun we have.
I pray it continues.

Thank You for the arguments,
even the ones when I am wrong,
each one enriches us
and the circle of love becomes stronger.

We have had to work hard at marriage, Lord.
There have been times when we have not
liked each other very well,
but we never quit!

Lord, when You finally got our attention
and helped us focus our life together on You,
it all seemed lighter,
better, and easier.

It took us a while, Lord,
but we figured it out.
Marriage without You is empty, lost.

Thank You, Lord,
for my husband.
He is more than I dreamed of.
He is stronger than I thought.
He will always be my friend.

Amen

Praise for the Blessings of Life

Dear Father God, Jesus Christ, and the Holy Spirit,

I praise You and thank You today for this day,
set aside to remind me of all You do,
each moment of each day.

Thank You for the many mistakes made,
lessons learned, success through fire.
It is through the chaos that I see
Your peace, Lord.

I thank You for so many unasked answers to prayer,
wonderful parents, and unconditional love,
from both You, Lord,
and them.

I thank You for the precious gifts of my children
who in turn teach and humble me.

I thank You for family and friends
who love and guide me
through this maze called life.

I thank You for the sunshine,
the sounds and tastes of autumn calling.
It is so good to take in and appreciate.

Thank You, God,
for this day set aside to observe
the splendor of Your creation,
and the magnificence of all You have done for me.

Thank You God!

Amen

Mentors

Dear God,

Thank You for the people You have put in my life,
the mentors, teachers, preachers,
friends, and family.

Heavenly Father—
keep me fascinated,
rejuvenated, energetic
and joyful.

Help me to remember
the lessons I have learned from failure.
Keep me from quitting anything!

Fill me with tenacity,
and grace me with Your kindness and Your love.
Help me to pass it forward.

Thank You for lessons learned,
mistakes made and sins forgotten.
Help me with Your grace and deliverance
to mentor others—to teach, to preach,
to encourage, and to comfort,
with divine assistance and assurance.

To You, God, all glory and honor is Yours.

Amen

Thanksgiving

Dear God the Father, Jesus Christ, and the Holy Spirit,

Today I come to You in thanksgiving.
I thank You for Your presence in my life.
I trust in You, O God,
to guide my path,

I thank You that You hold me in the palm of Your hand.
I am never alone, You walk beside me,
see me through my many trials…always.

I thank You for my wonderful parents who never
stopped believing in me or loving me.
Guide and bless them, Lord!

I thank You for such a treasured mate,
who walks through fire for me, supports me,
and stands united with me.

I thank You for the precious gift of my children.
They are Yours, Lord,
given to me for such a time.
May I never lose sight of how special they are.

Please guide and bless my children.
Help me to remember
that in my abounding love
for my children, mate, and parents,
You, Lord, love them more!
May I be grateful for my time together with them.

I thank You, Lord, for my life.
Open my eyes to Your wisdom and carry me
through each day.

Amen

The Power of God's Word

There is great power in Your Word.
From the beginning was Your Word.
It created everything, and nothing exists,
that Your Word did not create.
Christ Jesus is the eternal Word.

The Word of God is my foundation,
what I know to be true.
Promises and guidance for a life,
based on faith.

Your Word, God, is history.
I learn from it and pray with it daily.
Its power clears obstacles from my path and
gives me access to Your mighty seat
through Your Son, Jesus Christ.

Your Word offers,
if I believe,
mercy, forgiveness, and the grace
to begin anew each day.

Let me pray Your Word.
Unleash its power and favor
on a life searching for more.
Wanting more of You, O God.

Let me pray Your Word, God,
so I can resource all of You,
to make me all of what You want me to be.

The power of Your Word, God,
is there for all,
who believe and trust and
know it to be true.

Help me to pray Your Word, daily,
stand on the promises revealed in it.
Search always and I will find,
truth and strength,
perseverance and patience,
all that I need, eternally.

Amen

Praise

Dear Father God,

Praise Your Holy Name.
Hallelujah, Almighty God,
who delivers and clothes me
with garments of salvation.

I praise You, God,
for Your constant provision of my soul,
for the moments I notice and those I do not.

I praise You for Your blessings of home,
spouses, children, friends
and most importantly, Your Word!

I praise You for Your guidance,
Your sanctification and grace;
so deeply needed.

I praise and thank You
for loving me and never
leaving me alone.

Amen

Salvation
Father God,
My heart aches for those who do not know You,
I pray for the chains of pride and stubbornness
I pray for open eyes
I pray the sword of Your Spirit will flay all doubt
You, God, are the God of the impossible!
Help me to reach those who seem unreachable
May I, by my love for them,
Draw them near to You, Christ Jesus.
May my every breath in this life
Amen

Thankfulness

Dear God the Father,

Today is Your day,
I thank You for it!
I am Your child,
thank You for choosing me.

This world You created,
I praise You for Your beautiful creation.
I pray others will notice it.

Today and tomorrow,
I pray to serve You,
to notice You in every detail,
every word.

Please forgive my continual selfishness.
Help me to be obedient in prayer
and the study of Your Word.
Give me the knowledge of Your presence.

Open my heart and mind today and everyday
to You!

Amen

What Can God Do?

What can You do, God?
I know that everything is possible to those I believe.
If I trust in You and pray over all my burdens,
worry will cease and faith will reign.

My strength will increase and restoration will take hold.
You God, are my God of peace.
You reign with wisdom and
You give me that wisdom freely, if I ask.

What can You do, God?
You can do more than I ask or even dream of,
infinitely beyond my highest prayers, desires,
thoughts, or hopes.

You are the God of perfect peace,
You give me that peace when I trust in You
and keep my thoughts fixed on You.

What can You do, God?
You are the mighty conqueror.
You make all of my enemies
lie at peace with me.

You, God, are everything I need.
You guide me in all that I do.
You provide, if I seek Your kingdom first,
and make it my primary concern.

You guide me along the right path.
You have wonderful plans for my life.
You bless me when I patiently endure testing.
You guard me from the evil one.

What can You do, God?
Anything and everything,
if I put my trust in You,
seek You, be still and listen to You,
follow You, all the days of my life.

Amen

This Day

Dear Father God,

As this day begins,
I thank You for the gift of life.
I am in awe that You chose me and thought my life
was worth saving.
I praise Your Holy Name!

As this day begins,
may I see each tiny miracle and every big moment
that You have created for me.
I pray I will stop and notice all
the big and small things You have put in my world.

As this day begins,
I pray I will utter only Your divine words,
that my behavior would be disciple-like.
I pray to speak with the insight of
Your Holy Spirit's wisdom in love and friendship.

I pray that each day,
others will see the joy in me that comes
from my faith and trust in You.

Keep me from temptation, Jesus,
from harm and evil.
Guide my steps to be godly
and help me to strengthen my focus on You.

I pray that each day I will
reflect what I believe and hope to become.
In Your Holy Name, Jesus Christ.

Amen

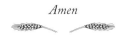

I Am Precious to Him

Dear Lord,

I pray I will remember that I am precious to You
because I abide in You, Christ,
and You abide in me.
My body is Your Holy Temple;
my efforts are Your Holy Spirit's work in my life.

May I always tremble at the magnificence of Your Word
and maintain a humble and contrite spirit.

May I focus on You, who is my authority
and is in ultimate control of this world!
Enable me to stand strongly on the rock of Your promises.

Help me to be Your child of God.
I know Your Word is action and
what You command, You accomplish.
I need to believe it!

May I live my life in gratitude, not believing
what others think,
but vulnerable and open to all possibilities of a life
lived in You.

God, please change my negative thoughts,
attitudes, and motives.
I owe You a great debt, Lord,
for forgiving my sins and loving me always.
Help me to respond to such debt by loving others freely,
regardless of the cost.

I pray I will live my life conscious of my place
in Your Kingdom.
I will remember that You love me,
that I am important to You,
that I am worthy!

Help me to seize that love from You, Lord,
and I pray through my use,
it will multiply and spread to the world.

Amen

Circle of Faith

Dear Lord,

I thank You, that we are all connected.
One prayer request for a friend, of a friend, who also
is a friend of another friend.
By our belief, in the power of prayer,
we are united, all attached to the vine,
held together by faith.

Peace is our promise, of prayer said for us,
and by us, for each other!
This community of believers,
who by our very presence,
hold each other up righteously,
to Your Holy Alter, God.
And we know, You have heard, You will answer…
Are we listening?

This community of believers,
this circle of faith, is how You, God, created us to be.
Meeting one another, lifting each other up.
Coming together in love,
love for You, and for one another.

This circle of faith, You have given us,
is such a gift of united existence.
For one cause, one belief,
that lightens hearts and lifts loads, burdens.
It is in the knowing we are never alone,
that makes the circle stronger
and the load lighter.

This circle, God, You created it.
We believe in it. Count on it.
Stand strong in it, and through our faith,
make it last from generation to generation.

Amen

Fall

Breathe

Breathe, just breathe,
then believe,
always believe.
Hope, don't ever lose hope.
Have faith, stand on it!

Breathe, in and out,
concentrate on the blessings,
don't look at the distractions.
Hope in the future,
make plans.

Breathe, keep breathing.
All my prayers have been heard…
they will be answered by Your glory and Your grace.
You are my Rock, my Refuge, and my Strength.
I will stand ready.

Breathe, I will survive this.
I will see the light.
I will feel Your love, Your peace.
Your peace will enfold me,
strengthen me for what is to come…
Breathe.

Amen

Complaining

Lord, I have been complaining again
about those circumstances
that I believe You have forgotten,
that seem unchangeable.

I feel despair and guilt over my grumbling,
yet I continue to pray for change.
Hope for a different outcome.

My groaning and complaining does not help.
It just keeps the focus on the negative,
on the difficult.

If I really am a believer,
not a doubter;
if I really trust in Your Word,
put all my hope in it,
then I need to look at this situation
much differently.

I need to stop repeatedly complaining.
I give You the burden, Lord,
and believe You have heard it.
You deliver me,
in Your timing and in Your way.
Believe in prayers heard, answers received.

These answers may not be what I expected, but…
You, Lord, are full of surprises.
Full of love for those who seek You.

The most important thing I can do
is to keep praying, looking to You, Lord,
repenting of my sins.
Believing, really believing, I am forgiven.

Looking to You,
staying close to You in prayer and in Your Word,
changes will come, almost impossibly,
to my circumstances…to me.

Thank You, Lord,
that I can complain and groan to You,
that You love me and forgive me.
You have unlimited mercy and compassion for me.
I will rest in it!

Amen

Defeat-Rejection-Reconciliation

O, Father God,

I pray that with every difficulty and trial in my life,
You will help me to wipe out the bitterness
of defeat or rejection.

I know life is not fair, Lord,
but I know You are in charge.
I give you my life completely,
to guide me down your path.
Show me Your way, light the lamp.
Help me to be obedient!

I pray for self-control, Lord,
it is so very hard to achieve.
I pray for hope and joy. I long to rest in Your peace.

People will fail me, Lord.
Help me not to be surprised but energized to be Your child…
full of mercy, forgiveness and hope!

I want to be firm in my faith,
quick to confess, repent fervently.
Forgive me, Lord,
and help me to forgive myself.

I pray for reconciliation, restoration and jubilation!
I pray I will sense Your perfect timing
and stay close to You, always!

May I never stray far from You, Lord.
May my faith grow like a mustard seed
to move Your mountains.

To Your glory, O Lord, I praise Your Holy, Holy Name.

Amen

Draw Near To God

O, Lord God,

I long for the courage to draw near,
to enter the Holy of Holies.

I pray I will be able to empty my sinful self
and be filled with You, Christ.

I hunger to be filled with Your peace,
Your presence,
Your path of purpose.

The world interferes.
It constantly intrudes rudely…
wanting my time and busyness,
taking me away from You.

Give me the courage, the brave spirit,
to combat earthly desires with heavenly pursuits.

Keep me pure and blameless with the
goal of pursuing Your likeness.
Focusing on trusting in You, God!

Your promises, God,
keep my faith unwavering.
I stand on Your foundation,
my foot firm in what I know to be true!

Give me the courage, Lord,
to enter the Holy of Holies.
Keep me focused on the prize.
Help me to stay true to the path You have chosen.

Amen

Guide My Children

Dear Father God, Jesus Christ, and the Holy Spirit,

I pray for my children,
that they know You as the Lord of their lives,
the director of their paths.

I pray that You guide them, Lord,
to encouraging friends,
a school where they will grow and prosper,
a believing mate,
a career that serves You,
and a lifestyle that glorifies You.

I pray that by my example,
they will learn of faith delivered,
trials endured, and sins forgiven.

I thank You, Lord,
for my children.
They are so precious in Your sight,
although challenging at times.
I pray for Your wisdom and direction,
that You are the focus in their lives,
and that these gifts, my children,
learn, love and become more like You.

As You gave them to me,
I give them back to You.
To hold in the palm of Your Hand
and guide them with Your Holy Spirit.
Hold them tightly in Your embrace.

I love them so dearly, Lord,
help me always to remember,
You love them more!

Amen

Humble Heart

Dear Father God,

I pray for a humble heart,
one that stays permanently focused on You!

I pray to remember, Lord,
all that You have done for me.
I am not worthy,
nor will I ever live up to my expectations
of what I want to be for You!

With Your guidance and wisdom,
I will follow Your path,
praying to never stray—
learning from my sins, praising Your Holy Name,
seeking the good for Your kingdom,
drawing near to You.

I pray, Lord,
for strength of character and integrity
amidst a world that does not value it.

I pray for faith and trust
when Your ways seem blind to me.

I pray for fortitude and perseverance
when I do not have a solution or answer—
just faith…
and just You!

Thank You, Jesus,
for this day, these circumstances,
this time in my life.
May my presence on this earth
bless Your Holy Name forever!

Amen

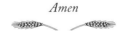

Indecision

Dear Jesus,

I look to You for direction.
I am at a crossroad
not knowing which way You want me to go.
You whisper to my soul,
I am God;
Your deliverer, protector,
director, father, friend, encourager.
Be still…wait,
you will find the path I direct you to
when My timing is perfect!
Do not be impatient.
Do not step out on your own!

Dare to dream the dreams I send to you.
Open up to levels you are not quite comfortable with.
If you let me,
I will stretch your spirit and belief
with many possibilities.

My hopes and dreams for you
are determined by your choices.
Take the time to be with Me.
Make Me important in your life.
Let your life reflect what you believe.

Believe in Hope not fear!
Stand in faith, not negative cynicism.
Rise in right thinking, I am always victorious!

I died for you. I will fight for you!
I will direct your paths.
Trust Me. I chose you.
My sacrifice shows My love for you!

Indecision is not inadequacy;
it is waiting on Your divine guidance and strength
to live my life worthy of the You, Lord,
who gave Your life for me.

So I am waiting…
I am being still,
ready to be led in the paths set before me
in righteous and hopeful expectation.

Amen

Lack of Devotion Time

Dear Father God, Lord Jesus Christ, and the Holy Spirit,

Forgive my lack of devotion and time for You.
Lord, I love You so much and want so dearly
to spend quiet time with You each day,
but life, children and husbands get in the way.
Forgive me, Lord!

Lord, forgive me for not giving that extra hug
to someone who needed it!
For angry words and thoughts,
for thoughtlessness, for lagging behind and not forging ahead.

Dear Lord Jesus,
today I want to take the time to pray,
to listen, and to feel Your presence and guiding spirit.
I want to notice You in the details,
and know You are always with me.

Forgive me, Lord,
for underestimating Your presence in my life.
I pray my joy that comes from knowing You,
will spread to others.
That my insufficiency will guide my dependence
on You and encourage my spirit to grow and soar.

Today, Lord,
Help me to take the time to feel Your peace,
grow in contentment and joy,
follow You faithfully,
and walk the path set before me!

Give me Your strength to boldly go forth in faith today!

Amen

Pray Without Ceasing

Pray without ceasing,
ask and you will receive.
These are Your words, God.
Why do I not believe them?

I doubt, fear, and walk without confidence;
lost, searching, pleading for Your help.

I am so busy begging and crying out to You,
that my anxiety builds,
the focus is on myself, not on You.

Refocus, clear my vision.
Let me see You;
help me not to look down
but to concentrate on You.

Keep me balanced.
Remind me of Your blessings.
Let me bask in gratefulness, see the cup as overflowing.
Lead me to Your world of peace.
Contentment and hope in the promises You have made to me, fulfilled.

Fill me with Your presence,
joy in every part of Your creation,
within me and the world around me.

Open my mind,
keep it clear and alert to every moment, every miracle,
in which You reveal Your presence to me.

Pray without ceasing, ask and you will receive,
concentrate on joy and be filled,
Hope…Believe.

Amen

Practice Forgiveness

Practice forgiveness, Lord?
Are You sure?
That person has hurt me
beyond what is reasonable.

Practice forgiveness! I prefer vengeance,
You say vengeance is Yours.
You have expectations for me,
to have mercy and to love others.

I am to forgive those hurtful words,
the deeds done for harm.
I am to practice forgiveness.
Seven times seventy, I am to forgive.
Compassion and grace are to be my foundation.

You say, Lord, for me not to judge others,
so I will not be judged.
I want Your unlimited love,
unfailing grace forever, not judgement.

You see, Lord, I am not worthy.
I know I have sinned.
Begging Your forgiveness, I learn of Your mercy,
The bitterness of unforgiving is not an option.

I pray for Your strength,
Your perseverance and Your continued ability
to forgive and let go of all hurts.
To concentrate on the good, and pull out the positive.

When I practice forgiveness, I live in peace.
Anger has no foothold,
depression, no seed.

I will practice forgiveness,
and learn to make it a habit.
Concentrating on the blessing,
I will walk closer to You, claiming my inheritance.

Practice forgiveness, Lord.
Reassurance of Your love received.
Mercy and grace lived out in a life anointed by You.

Let me practice forgiveness,
unlimited, unmerited,
as You do for me!

Amen

Stay Close to God

Holy Father God,

Let me learn the lessons of David, Lord,
how to stay close, dependent on You.
Never let me stray away
from Your glorious word or precepts.

May I begin each day thinking of You,
of all that You have done for me!
I pray I may serve You joyfully,
full of the fruit of the Spirit,
practicing self-control.

As I know temptation will come,
let me stand strong against it, recognizing it
and disarming it with Your Word and my faith.

I pray I will not disappoint You, Lord!
But I know I will!
When I do…
restore me and help me to learn from my sins
and repeat them no more!

As Your forgiven servant,
give me the words to evangelize, to love,
and bring the kingdom near to others.

Enable me, with only the power that comes from You, Lord,
to serve You, love You, praise You, and
be fruitful, for Your sake.

May You, God, send Your Holy Spirit to
guide me with discernment and wisdom
for this day and every day!

Amen

Self-Control

Dear Lord,

Oh, how I long to practice self-control.
It is the toughest characteristic of the fruit of Your Spirit,
I just can't attain it.

I struggle and pray, wrestle with failure, and give up…
hoping tomorrow I will do better.

Thank You, Lord,
for the lesson of Your Word,
scripture sent at this moment,
at this time,
for me to finally get it, receive it,
and live it.

It is not by my own power that I am to live in—
It is by Yours!
I can never practice self-control through my own determination,
only from Your power above.

When I finally pray for You, Christ, to indeed live in me
and meditate on Your Word,
then I am directed by Your Holy Spirit.

I am filled with Your peace
because I have let You, Christ, be my Prince of Peace.
I have become obedient
and hold every thought captive to You.

By the power of Your Holy Spirit, I am self-controlled.
I have begun to live in You,
for nothing is impossible through Christ
who gives me strength.

Strengthen me with Your Holy Spirit,
that I will, from this day forward,
be fruitful and self-controlled,
forever expressing Your love and being obedient to Your will.

Amen

Servant-Hood

Help me, Lord,
to put the strength of Your Word
into the actions of today.

Help me to walk, wearing Your armor, God.
To discern what is right or wrong,
to obey Your guidance,
to follow Your path.

Help me, Lord,
to help others!
To smile from my heart,
to love with Your love,
to bear fruit in Your kingdom.

As I walk Your earth,
let my mind dwell only on Your love and sacrifice,
not on the busyness of this world.

Apart from You, Lord,
I can do nothing!
With You, Lord,
and the faith of a mustard seed,
I can move mountains!

Help me to move mountains, Lord!

Come Lord Jesus!

Amen

Success God's Way

Dear Holy Father God,

Almighty is Your name!
Holy is the ground You walk on,
Sacred is Your Word.
Strengthened I am by Your presence.
Guided I am by Your purpose.

I pray for deliverance, success and hope,
for forgiveness of my fears,
doubts, excuses, procrastination, greed,
lack of conscience and laziness.

Help me to search Your Word,
seek Your peaceful presence,
and give all my burdens, every detail,
to You!

I will reside in hope.
Give, to keep the focus off myself,
be a witness to Your glory,
learn from my failures,
be humble in my successes.

The truth of Your Word lives in my heart.
Grant that I may live each day
in truth with joy.

Amen

Temptation and Cleansing

Dear Lord Jesus,

I pray You will keep me from the pit of sin
and sudden gratification.
Keep me honorable to You.
Help me to live with great endurance, self-control.

Help me to make the right choices.
Guide me to give all authority, all direction,
and all focus to You, Christ Jesus.

Help me not to isolate myself,
but to surround myself with fellow believers
who will hold me accountable to You.

I pray I will depend on You, Lord,
because only You can keep me safe.
You are my security, my home.
Keep me close to You.

When I draw closer to You,
I come back to a place where You
can bless me, Lord,
once more.

I repent of all my sins of thought, word, and deed.
Please, Lord, wash away my iniquities
and cleanse me with Your mercy.

Center in me, Lord, a clean, renewed,
and restored heart and soul,
so that I may be Your honorable and humble servant
now and forever!

Amen

Mistakes–Stumbles

Dear God,

Thank You for mistakes made,
lessons learned.
Help me not to repeat them again.

I so want to be Christ-like.
I despair of the humanness in me.
I long to stay in the safe harbor
of Your Word and prayer.

It is in that place I feel loved
and tremendous peace—
the cocoon that holds me close to You.

I dread my daily facing the world
of decisions and demands.
So, I will put on my armor, God,
stand firm and surely stumble
and make mistakes, again.

Thank You Lord, for picking me up,
yet again, dusting me off,
and sending me back filled with Your Holy Spirit
to face the challenges of another day.

Fill me with the energy necessary,
a positive attitude
and the joy of Your Spirit.

Amen

Watch Over My Child

Dear God,

My child is leaving my home, growing up and moving out.
These are the appropriate steps, at the right time.
I do not doubt, Lord, my child is ready,
but I know he is scared; So am I!
Fear is my enemy.

Lord, so many prayers have been sent up each day
for this child,
so many answered.
Continue to watch over this one.
I gave him to You from the beginning.

Thank You, God,
for such a gift, a blessing to raise.
Turn my fear of his future into faith for a safe tomorrow.
Guide him down the paths You choose.

He is Your child, Lord.
I pray he will glorify You through his life.
I pray he will love others and forgive as You do.

He is full of hope and adventure.
Send Your angels to help him succeed.
I pray he will always know, that his life
will not be successful on his terms,
but as a result of the answered prayers
from You.

May my child serve and worship You all the days of his life,
then my life, Lord, as Your servant,
has been all it was meant to be.

Watch over my child, dear Lord.
Keep him safe, help him to succeed, grant him wisdom,
guard his heart and soul.

Thank You, Lord,
for helping me raise this child.
Guide us both through this final stage.
Help us to be good to one other and love each other.

Thank You, Lord,
please continue to watch over my child.

Amen

The Throne of Grace

As I approach the throne of grace,
a prodigal son humbled,
hoping that once again forgiveness and mercy
will be mine to claim.

I am so unworthy.
My acts so unthinkable,
that grace seems out of reach…
unfathomable.

Your throne of grace speaks to me,
beckons me with love and acceptance…
mercy undeserved.

Your throne of grace renews my spirit,
adjusts my direction.
My focus becomes clear.
I exist because You deem it.
My existence is for Your pleasure.

The creation of life, of all things,
reigns on Your Throne of Grace.
How I approach it, determines my destiny.
I long to kneel at the throne of grace,
standing in the path of Your gaze.

Praise will flow unceasingly from my lips,
Your Throne of Grace has been my salvation,
my redemption, my cause in this life.

All honor, glory, and praise to You, God,
for giving me the blessing, the privilege,
the opportunity to approach Your Holy Throne of Grace.
Hallelujah!

Amen

Winter

Alone

Lord, today I feel so alone
as though no one has ever
experienced these trials,
these endurable contests of life.

Today Lord—
my aloneness enfolds me,
strangles me,
until I cannot take any more.

At that exact moment,
I reach for You and remember…
Your mercy, Your presence.

I remember You are my champion, defender,
physician, counselor, coach,
best friend, an eager listener,
and safe refuge.

My life is only bearable with You
as the foundation,
the beginning, the focus.

My joy is found in a life lived in Your presence,
practiced with Your peace,
and given with Your love.

Amen

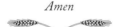

Anger

Dear Father God,

I beseech the help of Your Son,
Jesus Christ,
and I invite the intercession of Your Holy Spirit
into my soul.

Dear God, I am so angry. I know it is wrong.
I want to control every detail of my life.
I cannot! When I do, all goes wrong.

Dear God,
I want so badly to patch everyone's hurt,
put a band-aid on it
and have it stick.

I am unable to do all that my heart desires,
but I can give every burden to You.
I can do nothing without You, God,
but with You, all things are possible.

I pray the impossible!
The lost would be found.
The angry would find peace.
The silent would find solace.
That all would know You by name,
Savior, Joy, Lord of their lives!

I give You my anger,
my burdens, my pain.
I ask that You fill me with Your peace,
presence, direction
and then it will be all counted gain.

Dear Lord,
help me to remember You are in charge
and You have a plan
and that my part is to be faithful.

Thank You, God,
for listening, caring, and guiding.
Let my service reflect Your glory,
that my life be an example
of Your forgiving grace.

Amen

Trust in the Lord

I am empty Lord,
lost and depleted.
I am clinging to Your cross,
hoping for answers to all my questions,
longing for the peace of Your steadfast presence,
but feeling empty, lost.

I know in the midst of trial and tribulation,
it is best to praise You, trust in You,
the Creator of the Universe.

You know the plan.
Hold me close, O Lord,
You will guide me, deliver me.
Hold me close, Lord,
in the shelter of Your wings.

I will be still, waiting expectantly!
Patience will be my foundation,
mercy and forgiveness will follow.
Your Holy Spirit fills me
and peace reigns in my heart and mind.

I trust You, Lord God, for the next step,
I rest in Your arms.
I know the truth.
You are with me to the ends of the earth.
You will never leave me.
You have plans for me —
to serve, to love, to hope
and to help others.

I rest in the assurance of Your plans.
I hope in Your promises, Lord.
Hope does not disappoint.
I am still…
waiting on You,
Your peace reigns.
I am still…
it is well,
it is well within my soul.

Amen

Help Our Nation, Help Our People

Dear Father God, Jesus Christ, and the Holy Spirit,

I pray for help in our time of great need!

I pray for strength as a nation,
to be strong in what is right
and what You have ordained,
and clear on what is evil, wrong, or crushing.

Free me individually and us as a nation,
to help and love others,
without thought to selfishness.

Help me, Lord,
return to serving You joyfully
without thinking of consequence
but relying on Your provision, protection
and guidance.

Turn me individually and us as a nation,
to be Your people
who worship You with anticipation.
Help me to celebrate Your creation
and bask in Your love.

I look to You individually and us as a nation,
for wisdom and guidance with those whom we touch
so that we may survive this battle
and learn from our mistakes.

Let our nation never take our lives, families, friends,
churches, or country for granted!
Protect us, Lord!
I praise Your Holy Name, Father God!
I seek Your face and pray for victory
and peace in Jesus name.
I pray that in the practice of my faith,
I will remember You have heard me.

I pray to grow spiritually
and to serve You, joyfully!

Amen

I Surrender

I surrender my heart, Lord
come inside…
change me.
I pray Your position will refocus
my life and my priorities.

I pray to never let someone walk
unencouraged, uninspired,
or unfilled by the hope and joy
I have because of You.

Let my faith be evident to everyone I encounter!
Let it so radiate from me that I cannot contain Your light,
let it overflow, touching everyone.

I surrender this life to Your promised eternal life.
I look forward to the rewards
for a job well done,
by Your faithful servant.

I surrender!

Amen

God's Peace

How I cry for Your peace, O God,
rest and assurance have me yearning
for relief from worry and doubt.
Peace that only comes from You.

Unbelief comes knocking
persistently shooting arrows
into every corner of my mind.
It is a battle!

I cry to You, O God.
I cry for rest and peace,
a respite from worry and fear.
Unbelief attempts to set up residence.

I know my unrest is lack of focus on You, God.
Your Sabbath rest beckons me,
believing, trusting in the promises of Your Word.

I pray for relief, for rest.
Crying out to You for assurance,
craving the love You give,
wanting that love to fill every empty space.

God, Your Word promises that Your love,
Your peace and even Your joy will reside in me
through Your Holy Spirit's faithful presence.
Hope comes to live and casts out my worries, fears, and doubts.

I must press on and focus
on the promises in Your Word.
Ceasing thought of anything negative.
Working and focusing on the positive.

My expectations need to be hopeful.
I know, God, You love me.
You have wonderful plans that cannot be delivered,
stunted, halted by my unbelief.

I come to You, God,
pleading for rest, peace, and Your joy,
when I keep my thoughts fixed on You.

Amen

Life is Difficult

Why is everything so difficult?
I feel as though a black cloud follows me everywhere I go
What's next is my mantra!

I wonder if it is spiritual warfare or just the way life is?
I look at others and envy their carefree attitudes,
their confidence and joy.

I cry out to You, God, for relief, direction, hope;
You have been silent…no answers…just silent.

Then I realize…It's not all about me!
It is about helping and giving to others,
looking up and out, not down,
changing the pattern.

You are working to change me even before
You begin to change my circumstances.
Help me to keep my mind on You,
on Your path, not my own.

You want me seeking You first and foremost,
dwelling on the best in this life.
What is good, loyal, honorable, true, and right.

Bad things happen!
Spiritual warfare surrounds me!
But victory is mine, when You are my God!

I claim the shelter of Your wings.
You are my shepherd;
from now on, I shall not want.

It is not all about me;
it is about Your plans for me.
Your vision, goodness and mercy,
will follow me all the days of my life.

Amen

Lost Footing

Help me to find my footing, Lord, I am so lost.
I have left the shelter of Your wings
and tried again to fly out on my own.

The gravel under my feet is loose.
I remember the firm foundation on which
You have established me and right now—
it is gone and I am lost and afraid.

I search for You and find moments of peace.
It is not the long season of intimacy, of closeness,
that I desperately long for!

Help me to find my footing, Lord,
get back to the roots that I believe and know for certain.
Fill me with Your overflowing peace,
so that I know You are watching over me.

Guide me back to Your Holy Spirit,
and see the path and new purpose,
You have set before me.

Gracefulness, Lord,
I stand on what You have done before,
on what You are doing now,
and Your future blessings.
Help me find my footing, Lord,
again!

Amen

Prayer for a Child Who Has Lost Faith

Father God, Jesus Christ, and the Holy Spirit,

I pray for this child,
You know their struggles
and my disappointments.

Lord, I am so tired of trying to guide them when
they will not listen or when they completely step out
of Your will (according to me).
My fear for their future is a stumbling block
that works against my faith.

So, Lord,
in my quest to never stop learning or growing in faith,
I pray for this child.
Not my result-oriented prayers
but Your Will, in Your timing,
for their life and purpose under Heaven.

I pray that You, God,
will help me to hold up the shield of faith
against all fear and disappointment that I may feel.
I pray that my faith in their future,
will grow stronger more unbendable, unbreakable!

I pray that You, God,
will send positive faithful people
who will help them to recognize their gifts
and validate their faith.
Help them to grow in confidence
and enable them to be the great person of faith
that You want them to be.

I pray that Your armies in Heaven,
will fight for direction, purpose,
and success for this child.

I pray that my faith will set me free from my fear for this child.
Enable them through my faith
and Your battle…
to be all that You desire them to be.

Amen

Prayer for an Unbeliever

O, Lord,

I pray for _____,
that the walls will break down,
the shell crack open and they will let you in.

_____ is so lost,
so marred in the unbalanced.
Unfocused on what is real and who You are.

I pray for _____ to see You clearly.
Help them to find joy in the every day, the mundane,
to appreciate the smallest gift,
see the grass instead of the weeds.

I pray for the movement of their heart
to align them to Your priorities,
gratitude for all that they've received,
and the desire to give back freely.

I pray this yearning of my heart is fulfilled
by Your supernatural power.
I trust in Your timing to do this
in their life.

I look forward to their future with You.

Amen

Prayer of Grieving

Today I am caught off guard by Your plan.
I don't understand why
a precious life is cut short,
according to my perception.

I know life and its trials are not
according to my timetable
but the wisdom of Your purpose.

I will miss this godly person that You sent to
guide and help me to understand You.

He is not sorrowful.
He is singing with the angels.
My pain is so selfish and so worldly.

Thank You for his presence in my life.
He was so much Your servant,
he was Your holy representative.
Thank You for Him.

Amen

Spiritual Battles

Dear God,

All around me I see Satan's destruction,
and it unnerves and frustrates me.

I call on Your power and the Blood of Your Son, Jesus Christ,
to be victorious in the lives of those I love
and those I am praying for.

Father God, please send Your Holy Spirit,
and all Your angels to win the spirituals battles
for these souls.

Reveal Your grace and mercy
to those who are unaware.
Take the scales off the eyes of those
who do not see and do not believe.

To those who believe, but are in the midst of battle,
I claim victory through Your Armor, God,
and the Blood of Your Son, Jesus Christ.
Send Your peace of mind, so worry does not rule
and anger has no foothold.

Enable me when in the presence of battle,
to be a fighter, to be bold in my beliefs,
and my foundations.

Hold up those I hold dear.
I claim victory for them,
and in perfect faith, I claim the peace
that surpasses all understanding.
Knowing God, that You are in charge…
even down to the hairs on their heads.

I claim victory in the Blood of Your Son, Jesus Christ.
I claim grace in the resurrection.
I claim peace in Your Holy Spirits presence…
Now and Forever.

Amen

Sin

Dear God,

My sinfulness is showing again.
Try as I might,
I step off the path right into what I know is wrong.
Anger becomes my friend,
I feel righteous in it even though I know it is wrong.

I pray for wisdom…
huge doses please!
I am humbled over and over again.
It is good to be humble,
it lets go of pride.

I pray for guidance, wisdom,
and the direct intervention of Your Holy Spirit.
You say in Your word to ask, seek,
and it will be given to You.
I am asking, seeking, and banging on that door!

Thank You, God, for listening to me,
loving me when I am most unlovable,
and gently guiding me back
onto Your path of righteousness.

Thank You above all, for showing me
that even at my worst,
You still love me,
and that You will still fight for me
in this spiritual war on earth.

You are my rock, my strength, my defender,
my physician, and my counselor.
Please nail my sins to Your cross and help
me to learn from them and repeat them no more!

Amen

Suffering

Dear Lord,

There is so much suffering,
I do not understand.
Lives shortened by illness You have not healed,
even when many, many petitions have been sent.

Lives shortened by tragic events, accidents—
Why Lord? Why them?
I so want to understand the reasons, the timing.

Lord, I know there is evil in the world,
but I want You to conquer it all, right now!

It all comes down to faith!
Faith like Job, that stands
no matter the circumstances.
Faith of a mustard seed that moves mountains,
my mountains of doubt and fear.

I live by faith, not by sight.
I cannot see the end,
but by faith, I know the end,
eternity with You and those I love.

Faith…so deep
that when doubt creeps in and fear shouts,
I stand firm knowing that You, Lord,
will work everything for Your good.
You have a plan for me,
to prosper and succeed.

I am Your child.
You love me more than I can imagine.
Your plans for me
are only possible, hopeful, if I have faith.

Amen

Unbelief-Doubt

Dear Lord Jesus,

Please help my unbelief!
I long to step out of doubt
onto the path of righteousness, goodness,
and the undeniable knowledge of what is right.
I yearn to know which way to go,
and what to do next.
May my faith grow beyond what I imagine
to what You have planned for me!

With Your wisdom, God,
help me accomplish and discern the right choices.
In the midst of criticism, cynicism
and negative influences,
I pray I remember that You, God,
are the one who holds me up and shelters me
beneath Your wings.

Do not let circumstances affect my faith!
My faith is completely reliant on my focus on prayer and
devotion time, with You!
May I stay close—
always, Lord!

Take away all of my selfish sins, Lord.
There are many!
I pray that I will be honest before You, God,
and You will forgive me!
I pray for Your mercy and I repent wholeheartedly!

I praise Your Holy Name for choosing me
and making me part of Your Holy Family!
I praise You and thank You for the joy that comes from
intimacy in prayer and study with You.

May I serve with hope and joy
May I choose the narrow,
path directed by You, God!
May I unabashedly explain to all who ask—
that the glorious salvation is mine
through Jesus Christ, Your Son,
the One and Only!

Amen

Victory With God

Dear Father God, Jesus Christ, and the Holy Spirit,

Help me, Lord,
not to fear, be frustrated,
experience hopelessness or panic.
Help me to focus my attention on You, Lord,
not on my battles.

I am powerless!
I claim Your promises.
I stand firm on the foundation of Your Word.
I put on Your Armor God, and wait on You, Lord…
my deliverer, my strength.

Help me remember Your sovereignty over everything!
I pray I will be accountable
and repentant always.
When all have deserted me,
help me to rise up out of the ashes of battle
into the victory that comes from finding my strength
and ability in You alone, God.

I remember victory does not mean an easy win,
but often one fought with great struggles.
But out of struggle and strife, comes strength,
fortitude, and reliance on You.

I pray my memories of kindness received
will stay with me forever
and that my offenses be washed away!

As I serve You, God,
as an armor-bearer in the battle
for what is right and true,
I pray for wisdom, guidance,
and deliverance.

Thank You, Lord God, for Your Word Promises;
the victory is assuredly mine.
As Your servant…
open my eyes to where I am to be…
for Your Glory.

Amen

Works vs God's Pleasure

Dear Lord,

I struggle so with my insecurities,
my wanting to make everyone happy,
provide and protect in my own power.
It does not work!

I struggle with my works,
those jobs I assume
with little desire and less time.
I want to impress You, Lord,
with my devotion.
It does not work!
Hopefully, someday soon,
I will really get it,
know in my heart and soul
that if I focus on You, Jesus,
if I live for You and Your kingdom,
grace, mercy and peace
are mine forever.

Fill me with Your power, Jesus,
to be righteous in Your eyes
because I love You
and want fervently to glorify You to others.
Help me to be a strong branch
attached to Your vine, Jesus Christ.

May I do nothing out of ambition
and everything to glorify Your Name and
Your presence in this world!

Amen

Cleansing Tears

Cleansing tears of forgiveness, of burdens.
Valleys where hurt is so deep,
Lord, it seems all I do is cry and beg you to rescue me.

My emotions are so close to the surface,
ready to explode at any given moment.
I long to be self-controlled, but I sin continually.

My sin brings tears
and my confession, my vow to do better,
sheds continuous self-condemnation.

I am so tired of it all!
Being joy-filled and spirit-led are my goals.
I continually fall short.
Lamentations are my focus!

Lord, I pray for You to help me with my tears,
to turn them to gratefulness and into joy focused tears.
Give me the perseverance and endurance
to redirect the emotions You gave me as a blessing to—
Bless You!

Give me peace, Lord, I beg You.
I seek the ability to use my emotions and practice self-control.
May I glorify You,
and make my life full of Your purpose.

Cleansing tears, Lord;
use them to mold and uphold me,
strengthen my resolve.
Faith through redemption.
Redemption through cleansing.
Cleansing to holiness.

Amen

Fear

Dear Lord,

Today I give You my fear.
I am afraid of the unexpected,
the unknown,
events of tomorrow.

Today, I give You my fear,
this heavy burden,
because I can no longer carry it!

I know, Lord, this fear,
it is not from You.
It is the measure and force
of the enemy coming to call.

I place my hand in Yours,
knowing by my faith and Your grace,
all will be well.

My soul longs for the peace promised by You.
I search and hope to find it.
Nothing can separate me,
Your loving servant,
from Your love,
not even my fear.

I give You my fear, Lord,
and I take Your hand in peace.

Amen